Multibillion
Translation & Interpretation:
The Future in Language Careers

Lynn Henry-Roach

For Chris, Christopher and Gabrielle,
and Marianne who inspire me.
Dad who taught me to be resilient.
Mother, the angel who watches over me.

Acknowledgments

My special thanks to Arleta D. for assisting me in the completion of this book.

To all my family and friends who have encouraged me to pursue my endeavors over the years, I thank all of you. It has meant so much!

This book is written for all who strive to make a difference in the lives of others who need our services as translators, interpreters, and ASL interpreters.

Table of Contents

Introduction

Preface

Let me start by saying that this book is not for everyone. If your focus is on getting technical advice on how to conduct a simultaneous interpretation, this is not what this book offers. Rather, this is a book that gives an overview of the translation and interpretation industry and the trends related to it.

This book is designed to help you jumpstart and grow your career. I am sharing my 25-plus years of experience for those who are willing and committed to upholding the professional standards and code of ethics for this industry.

This is meaningful and important work. Often, I am asked who should read and use this book. The answer is simple: those who want to begin or grow their career as a language interpreter, American Sign Language (ASL) interpreter, or translator. The prerequisite for this career path is to be proficient (fluent) in English and one or more other languages. Fluency, in this context, is defined and measured by one's ability to not only speak the language but to also read and write it and to understand the related culture(s).

My two decades plus of professional work experience and training have gone into the creation of this book. I hope you will benefit from my knowledge. I hope to save you time and money by offering you a comprehensive overview of this multibillion-dollar industry, and that you find the informational material interesting and helpful to your career.

About Me

So what's my story, and what makes me qualified to tell you about the interpretation and translation industry? It all started as a child when I emigrated at the age of three to the United States with my family from Haiti. We settled in a nice suburban area outside of Washington, D.C. called Silver Springs, Maryland. There I lived and started elementary school. Fortunately, both of my parents were able to continue working in their respective professions; my mom was a registered nurse, and my dad was an electronic engineer.

My parents encouraged us as a family to master the English language and, subsequently, we were able to assimilate into the American culture too. Years later, as an adult, I realized that many times professionals who have emigrated to the USA face obstacles in getting the American equivalent of their certifications, degrees, etc. that they held in their home country and that would have permitted them to continue their professional careers in the USA.

At home, I was exposed to several languages like French, Haitian-Creole, and English. I grew up as a heritage speaker, using English as my principal language, at first. However, starting in the fifth grade, I began studying French. I became a fluent speaker and went on to complete a double major at Rutgers University in French and Political Science. While at college, I studied French grammar, literature, history, and current events, and it was there that I first had the idea to have a career as an interpreter.

Now to give you an idea, it was the early 1990s, and there were few options for language majors, outside of teaching. The only career interpreters I knew at the time were the United Nations interpreters I had seen on TV. Upon graduation from college, I remember getting excited and dreaming about the possibility of working at the United Nations with all those international leaders and diplomats.

Sadly, I soon found out that it is not how you get to work at the United Nations or any other place. Being bilingual is a prerequisite for becoming an interpreter or translator, but it is not even close to being the only thing you need to have in your skillset or arsenal.

I share my background to help you understand that there are many factors involved in becoming a successful interpreter and/or translator in the USA.

These days, I am a French- and Haitian-Creole-speaking certified healthcare interpreter, linguist, language coach, language proficiency test administrator, test rater, guest lecturer, and now an author on the subject matter.

Education is very important to me, and in my work as an interpreter, I have been an advocate for the LEP (Limited English Proficiency) community having access to social services, education, and of course, healthcare.

In my career, I have long been an advocate for sharing information, services, and resources to all who ask me. Over the years, many have asked me:

- "How did you get your job?"
- "Where did you receive your training?"
- "How can I start my career as an interpreter or a translator?"
- "How can I get certified?"
- "Is there a lot of work in your field?"

Back in 1992, I was hired as a Haitian-Creole/English interpreter. This was my first official position as a paid interpreter and case manager for a non-profit agency in Newark, New Jersey. I was tested daily on my language on medical and legal terminology. I learned quickly that I had to brush up and acquire the vocabulary and keep up with culture in order to be effective in my job. This was my very first work assignment as a case manager/interpreter for these clients. I also learned about working with people who spoke the same language I did, but who had very different life experiences than my own.

Some were older, from the countryside, had low literacy levels, or were suffering from anxiety and other medical issues. I soon realized how culture is very relevant when talking about language too. So I had to get familiar with and understand my clients' backgrounds and worldview.

During the course of my twenty-plus-year career, I have worked as an interpreter and translator in various fields including medical, education, legal, courts, immigration, business, and social services industries. In each industry, I had to learn my way around it, including the terminology, laws, regulations, and industry trends. This required curiosity and persistence on my part.

In addition, in 2007, I started 4u Language Services, LLC, which specializes in multilingual translation and interpretation, and bilingual education. As a result, I have built a network of translators and interpreters across the USA. Worldwide, I am connected to thousands of like-minded professional translators and interpreters via LinkedIn, Twitter, and other social media. I am a proud small business owner. I started my own company so that I could have more flexibility and opportunities to work on the projects that interest me. My business has allowed me to further develop my skills and to learn how to expand my network and grow professionally. For me, it was a natural evolution, as I have always wanted to operate my own company. I figured out early on that I enjoyed being my own "boss."

Now, keep in mind that I worked for about thirteen years before I established my business. It is essential that you learn the business and work under the guidance of an established entity before you branch out on your own. I was fortunate in that I worked for public school districts and hospitals that were willing and able to provide their interpretation staff with the most current training in best practices. In addition, my employers also paid for some of my tests, such as the Oral Proficiency Interview (OPI) and Bridging the Gap Medical Training. And no worries...the OPI and medical training programs will be further discussed later in this book.

My credentials, education, and training include certifications as a nationally certified healthcare interpreter by C.O.R.E.-CHI. I have met the standard requirement set forth by the Georgia Department of Education to teach French in grades K-12, and Board Certified in School Crisis Response (BCSCR) as an interpreter to be on the front line with police, medical, law enforcement, administrators, and faculty in order to communicate with families and students during a school crisis.

As you can see, I have a diverse background in translating and interpreting, and I am also very passionate about helping others learn about this industry and how to get certified doing the work that you want to do. I get my sense of fulfillment in teaching others as well as learning from them. I have heard many times people say that you must be ready when opportunity knocks. So what does that really mean? It means you are ready to meet your destiny because you know what you want, who or where to find what you want, and how to obtain it because you have prepared. In other words, you have to do your homework to be successful.

This a competitive industry just like any profession. You have to work smart to reach the top. As you read this book, I suggest that you consider the various industries and ways that you can earn a lucrative career by learning all the ways you can offer your professional language services. (Salaries and work conditions will be discussed in future chapters.) You may consider combining your skills; for example, translation and foreign language interpretation, or perhaps American Sign Language (ASL) and translation.

Why You Should Read This Book

Why read this book? Read it if you can speak two or more languages fluently or know ASL. Read it if you want to join the fast track to better understand industry opportunities to a successful career as a translator or interpreter.

Often I am asked if you need a college degree to become a certified interpreter or translator, and the answer is "No, not necessarily." Keep in mind that each employer has their own requirements for hiring. But what I do know from talking to many employers over the years is that certification with little or no experience can be preferable to lots of work experience but no certification. The reason is that now many employers request certification to remain competitive in their area of expertise. The clients are also demanding certifications before they allow anyone to work on their projects. This is why I will place emphasis on getting certification, which is what will most likely get you hired with an employer and probably give you the ability to secure U.S. federal government contracts, along with other criteria.

Maybe you are a recent college graduate with a translation or interpreting degree. Or maybe you are an experienced veteran who needs to expand business with the goal of winning a bid on a U.S. federal government contract. Now is a great time to enter this fast-growing field. With the insider pointers I provide, you can save time and money by getting the information you need right away to help you achieve three key benefits:

1. Potentially double or triple your hourly income.
2. Have excellent schedule flexibility. Work from home on the phone or on a computer.
3. Give back to your community or make a difference in the life of an LEP. Do meaningful, fulfilling work, and earn great satisfaction in helping others.

This book is written for bilingual and multilingual individuals who want to become professional translators or interpreters. This information will be of special interest to students and teachers of foreign languages. In addition, ASL volunteer interpreters and native speakers of foreign languages can use this book as a resource guide to launch a meaningful and profitable career.

This industry has a high demand for workers, as projected by the U.S. Bureau of Labor Statistics. My hope is that you will find this information practical and that you will use this knowledge to jumpstart or expand your career. Here are some key points to note:

- ✓ The translation is written, and interpretation is spoken. They are two different skills, and they require different training.
- ✓ Being bilingual is not sufficient to make you a translator or interpreter. You need additional training to acquire specific skillsets.
- ✓ Translation is more than word substitution.
- ✓ Machine translation is not going to replace human translators.
- ✓ ASL interpreters are in high demand. In fact, ASL classes are being offered in high schools now, just like Chinese, French, Spanish, etc.
- ✓ And here are some tips to succeed in this profession:
- ✓ Know your native language well, including grammar and culture.
- ✓ Continue to improve your knowledge of your second language.

- ✓ Use the media, print, television, music, and radio to hone your listening, speaking, and writing skills.
- ✓ Start and grow your personal library of dictionaries (e.g., medical, legal, business, and other specialized areas).
- ✓ Build a glossary of terminology based on specific subjects.
- ✓ Be inquisitive, and ask questions about various global topics. Keep up with current events.
- ✓ Use the Internet, workshops, classes, and professional associations to network.
- ✓ Continue learning via travel, courses, seminars, and staff development opportunities at work.
- ✓ Be professional. Be on time, and dress conservatively.
- ✓ Follow the professional code of ethics issued by your state or follow federal guidelines.

In 2012, the Registry of Interpreters for the Deaf gave a more formal framework to the process of becoming a nationally certified interpreter, requiring aspiring hearing interpreters to have a bachelor's degree before testing. Other organizations, such as the American Translators Association and the International Association of Conference Interpreters, offer various forms of certification as well. Given the formal education, certification, and state regulations, becoming an interpreter and translator can be an involved process. While a formal education is becoming increasingly important, those seeking to enter the field must, above all else, be fluent in English and another language and have a minimum of a high school diploma.

Statistics About the Industry

The translation and interpretation industry is large and growing. Here are some industry statistics for translation services in the U.S. as of 2015[1]:

1. $5.8 billion in revenue in 2015
2. $1.5 billion in profit
3. $1.5 billion in wages
4. 53,691+ businesses
5. 3.4% to 4.9% annual growth rate (2010–2020)
6. 41.7% written translation services
7. 54.6% interpretation services
8. 3.7% Other

Check out the current statistics and job projections for 2016 to 2029: The field is on track to add 15,500 new positions during that period. As diversity in the U.S. increases and globalization continues at a breakneck pace, so will the demand for spoken-language interpreters. Job prospects are especially bright for those fluent in Chinese, German, Russian, Portuguese, and Spanish. Sign-language interpreters should also expect an employment boom, thanks to the popularity of video relay. The median annual wage for interpreters and translators was $51,830 in May 2019.

"In May 2019, the median annual wages for interpreters and translators in the top industries in which they worked were as follows:

Professional, scientific, and technical services	$57,450
Government	57,370
Hospitals; state, local, and private	50,980
Educational services; state, local, and private	50,110

Wages depend on the language, specialty, skill, experience, education, and certification of the interpreter or translator, as well as on the type of employer. Wages of interpreters and translators vary widely. Interpreters and translators who know languages that are in high demand or that relatively few people can translate often earn higher wages. Those who perform services requiring a high level of skill, such as conference interpreters, also receive higher pay.

Employment of interpreters and translators is projected to grow 20 percent from 2019 to 2029, much faster than the 4 percent average for all occupations. Employment growth reflects increasing globalization and a more diverse U.S. population, which is expected to require more interpreters and translators.

Demand for American Sign Language interpreters is expected to grow due to the increasing use of the video relay services.[2]

In addition, growing international trade and broadening global ties should require more interpreters and translators, especially in emerging markets such as Asia and Africa. The ongoing need for military and national security interpreters and translators should result in more jobs as well.

Computers have made the work of translators and localization specialists more efficient. However, many of these jobs cannot be entirely automated, because computers cannot yet produce work comparable to the work that human translators do in many cases to ensure that sentences and words are used in the proper context.

Job Prospects

Job prospects should be best for those who have at least a bachelor's degree and for those who have professional certification. Those with an advanced degree in interpreting and/or translation also should have an advantage and the potential for higher pay.

Typical Fees

"Wages depend on the language, specialty, skill, experience, education, and certification of the interpreter or translator, as well as on the type of employer. Wages of interpreters and translators vary widely. Interpreters and translators who know languages that are in high demand or that relatively few people can interpret or translate often earn higher wages. Those who perform services requiring a high level of skill, such as conference interpreters, also receive higher pay.

Self-employed interpreters usually charge per hour.

Half-day or full-day rates are also common.

Self-employed interpreters and translators often have variable work schedules, which may include periods of limited work and periods of long, irregular hours. Most interpreters and translators work full time.[4]

While projects and fees vary widely, it is helpful to know what some typical projects pay and how long they take.

An example would be working on a one- or two-page birth or marriage certificate where you could charge $50-$75 for doing the translation. You can also charge by the word for such projects, with a common range being between 12¢ and 27¢. The variance is due to how in-demand a language is, how technical the material is, and the turnaround time to complete the translation project. A "rush order" for a translation project can mean minutes, hours, or days. Therefore, it is important that the rates reflect the time, accuracy, and effort to complete by the translator.

If you're doing translation for a book, well then, that's a lot of words. You could have a flat fee for this project as you assess the page count or total word count. You can do this with romance novels, non-fiction books, and textbooks. Also, you can charge much more for technical documents because they involve a lot more expertise and work. The range can be a little bit higher because you may have to research some terminology to ensure the accuracy and quality of the translation.

Let's say that you have completed the first translation of a text. You would then work with an editor who would review the text and make sure that the context and the accuracy of the content have been preserved, in addition to verifying the correct use of grammar and punctuation. So it really takes two people to complete the translation.

Translation options are showing up all over the Internet right now, as more and more websites have multiple languages available. You can say, "Oh, I want to read this in French," and with just a couple of clicks, the page translates to French! Even on LinkedIn or Facebook, you can choose your language. So someone had to integrate the multi-language option. A translator collaborated with an IT person to get that facilitated, and it's now commonplace. It's also everywhere when you go to foreign countries in Europe, Asia, or Africa. Many places have at least two official languages, so everything must be presented in all the official languages. There might be two different billboards at the airport, for example, in English and French, English and Spanish, English and Portuguese, or even Dutch and German. So many people in Europe speak two or three languages, and certainly, in Africa, they speak three, four, or maybe five dialects or languages. It's commonplace.

Here are some notable international agencies that use more than one language for all communications:

1. Olympics – English/French/host country
2. General Assembly – United Nations General Assembly – English/French
3. European Union – English/French
4. IMF (International Monetary Fund)

The working language of the IMF is English. Other languages—mainly Arabic, Chinese, French, Russian, Portuguese, and Spanish—are used in the IMF's interaction with member countries. Local languages are often used in the field. A policy of disseminating information in languages other than English is in effect.

Nevertheless, the vast majority of IMF meetings are held exclusively in English, and most meetings that require interpretation use two languages only. With a limited number of staff interpreters, the organization relies heavily on freelancers.

Interpretation Services

"IMF Language Services is a group within the Corporate and Facilities Department. Language Services provides translation and interpretation services, both locally and abroad, to facilitate communication between the IMF, its member countries, multimedia, and the general public. Although the Fund maintains a core of staff translators and interpreters, a significant portion of the work is performed by freelancers based in the U.S. and around the globe. Interpretation Services has a roster of over 4,000 freelance interpreters in over 110 countries. [5]

Multilingualism and WHO (World Health Organization)

WHO's multilingual website, publications, and other resources ensure that health information reaches the people who need it, in the languages they can understand. This makes access to health information both more equitable and effective.

Multilingual communication bridges gaps and fosters understanding between people. It allows WHO to more effectively guide public health practices, reach out to international audiences, and achieve better health outcomes worldwide. In this way, multilingual communication is an essential tool for improving global health.

Six official languages

WHO's six official languages—Arabic, Chinese, English, French, Russian, and Spanish—were established by a 1978 World Health Assembly resolution turning multilingualism into a WHO policy. Since the adoption of the resolution, all governing body documents and corporate materials have been made available online in all official languages.

Many of WHO's key scientific publications—like the International Classification of Diseases, World Health Statistics, and the World Health Report—appear in six languages, and often many more.

The World Health Assembly's most recent resolution on multilingualism, adopted in 2008, repeats the call for linguistic diversity across the organization, and a five-year plan of action (2008–2013) has been underway to meet this challenge.[6]

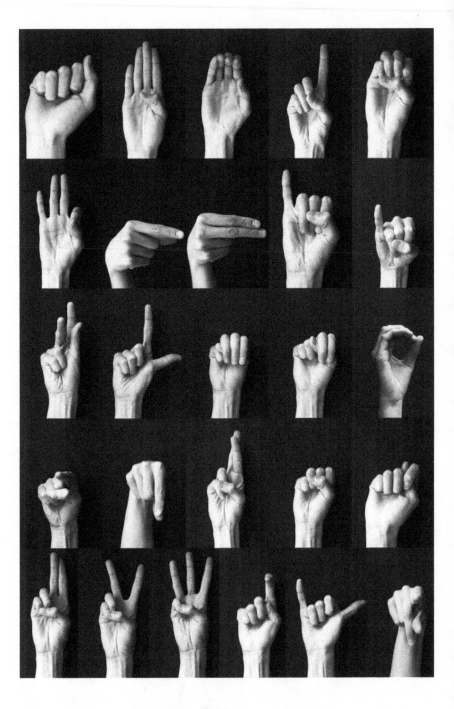

CHAPTER 1

Translation & Interpretation

Translation and Interpretation Defined

Interpreters and translators enable the cross-cultural communication necessary today by converting one language into another. However, these language specialists do more than simply translate words—they relay concepts and ideas between languages. They must thoroughly understand the subject matter in which they work to accurately convert information from one language, known as the source language, into another, the target language. In addition, they must be sensitive to the cultures associated with their languages of expertise.

Interpreters and translators are often discussed together because they share some common traits. For example, both must be fluent in at least two languages: a native language, or active language, and a secondary language, or passive language; a small number of interpreters and translators are fluent in two or more passive languages. Their active language is the one that they know best and into which they interpret or translate, and their passive language is one for which they have nearly perfect knowledge or proficiency.

Although some people do both, interpretation and translation are different professions. Interpreters deal with spoken words, translators with written words. Each task requires a distinct set of skills and aptitudes, and most people are better suited for one or the other.

While interpreters often work into and from both languages, translators generally work only into their active language. Interpreters convert one spoken language into another—or, in the case of sign language interpreters, between spoken communication and American Sign Language (ASL). This requires interpreters to pay attention carefully, understand what is communicated in both languages, and express thoughts and ideas clearly. Strong research and analytical skills, mental dexterity, and an exceptional memory are key.

Types of Translation and Interpretation Jobs

The full range of the different industries that use translators and interpreters is quite vast, and there is a wide variety of business and organizational jobs that require these services.

Literary

Literary projects require translators, but this is not limited to traditional textbooks and technical books. Such work can also involve websites, brochures, articles, journals, novels, textbooks, and print advertisements and signs, such as billboards.

Academic

Academic publications (journals and research) are often translated into different languages for use in different countries. Also, academic journal articles and similar items, such as posters, can be translated to give their authors a larger worldwide audience. Other items that often require translation are school forms, policies, IEPs (Individual Education Plans), and materials for parent/teacher conferences.

Legal

There is a large and growing need for legal translators and court interpreters all over the country (immigration, INS, ICE, TSA airport, deportation, and asylum hearings). There are many legal situations that require an interpreter be present by law, or that certain types of documents, such as contracts, be translated for non-English speakers, but there are also other untapped opportunities in this field for translators/interpreters, including ASL, working with independent law firms. Other opportunities include depositions, court appearances, interviews, and insurance claims, to name a few.[7]

Medical

The medical field is another where there is always a great need for skilled interpreters and translators. Medical crises and ongoing regular medical care provide numerous opportunities for interpreters and translators. Interpretation services are needed for clinic appointments, preoperative and postoperative care, heart care, dialysis, prenatal care, and pediatric clinics, etc.

Patients require help with understanding what is being said by medical professionals, and they also require help to complete medical consent forms, medical releases, and a variety of HIPAA policy-related and patient care documents.

Film/television

Film and television work can involve translating text in subtitles or even translating part of a dialogue being used in a script. Your work may include translating press releases, dubbing, ad promos, and voiceover talent for worldwide audiences.

Localization

Localization is where the language is translated into the local dialect, and it is used more frequently than you might realize. Among countries speaking the same language, and even within an individual country, there are often words that are unique to each region. The same word in each region can have an entirely different meaning, and this can lead to significant misunderstandings if the phrase, word, or sentence is not localized. A good example of this is with the Spanish language: many of the versions spoken around the world have some differences with nuances in the meaning of words and expressions.

Sight Translation

There is an interesting combination of translating and interpreting skills required for sight translation. Sight translation is where a short document is presented to an interpreter for them to read and translate orally on the spot. For example, if a patient had to sign a medical consent form before going into surgery, the interpreter would read the consent form and explain what the surgery risks are, how long the patient might be hospitalized, and what the policies and procedures are relative to patient care while in the hospital.

Machine vs. Human Translating and Interpreting

I am often asked about the ability of computers to efficiently translate. Some of the drawbacks are that computers lack human experience, and they have primitive artificial intelligence. They have no EQ (emotional quotient), and they are culturally insensitive.

There are many tools, such as Google Translate (and the related phone app) and software products and systems, such as Trados translation software, that translators can use to help them complete their work. While you cannot consistently rely on these tools, they can assist a translator sometimes when they need a quick definition for context, or as a thesaurus if they are stuck.

Commonly, the first time people use machine technology, they think, "Wow, this is the greatest thing ever!" That is until they read the translation. If you know the target language, you will soon realize that there can be problems with machine translation (MT).

The bottom line is that these tools work better if one already knows the language because of context.

Machine technology translations do have their advantages. They are fast. Some software can translate seventeen words per second, which is 61,200 words per hour. An experienced human translator can usually manage 650 words per hour.

Another advantage is that MT does not take creative license with a translation. A computer always translates the same word in the same way. However, it can also make the same errors multiple times if you do not correct it.

It's important to note that you need to be sure to change the tone after the software translation is produced to make the translation accurate.

Finally, MT is less expensive than human translation. Nevertheless, this can be deceiving because the price of the software is not the only consideration. You will always need an expert to review or check the MT. Always have an editing translator proofread for the final copy.

The limitations of MT (machine translation) are finally being acknowledged by those who make the software. They are now warning people to consider their translations as drafts.

Here are some instances when machine translations work well:

1. On the Internet. MT helps us get a general sense of the information we find online.
2. For technical publishing. Many companies use MT for preparing technical publications.

Common Misconceptions About Translating

"Translation is sometimes taken too lightly. Translation is, in fact, a serious business that should be approached sensibly to avoid poor communication, which can result in lost deals or even incite conflicts.

Before starting a project that involves translation, bear in mind the following misconceptions regarding translations".[8]

Misconception #1: If you know a foreign language, you can be a translator.

This is perhaps the most common translation misconception and the most damaging one. Being able to read, write, and speak a foreign language does not give anyone a license to undertake translation work, although these are fundamental prerequisites.

A translator must have an in-depth understanding and knowledge of at least two languages: a foreign language and a mother tongue.

Translating is a skill. You must be able to write well and have an excellent command of the nuances in language use.

Be aware that language is not free of cultural influences. Context is relevant, and localization is important.

Misconception #2: Translating is easy.

Translation is far from easy. It can be very intricate and arduous work. Having to simultaneously concentrate on two different texts is mentally exhausting, as a translator is continuously moving between two languages and frames of mind.

A translator must first read and register source information, and then manage to digest it and present it accurately in the target language. This means having an excellent vocabulary and appreciating the subtleties in language, such as phrases, metaphors, tone, and intention.

Misconception #3: Computers can now do translations.

No machine translation can or ever will be able to take the place of human translators. This is because computers do not understand what language is, how it is used, the subtleties within it, and the ever-changing use of it.

Computers may be able to translate simple, one-dimensional sentences, but they will never be able to tackle the complexities within literature or technical texts.

Misconception #4: Having a professional translation is not crucial.

If the translation is to be accurate and professionally prepared and presented, then an experienced translator is crucial.

Bad translations lead to many problems and misunderstandings, which ultimately reflects poorly on a company or organizational brand.

CHAPTER 2

How to Be Successful

Qualities of a Successful Translator or Interpreter

Translating and interpreting require several skill sets, and the work can be demanding. However, the required skills can be learned, and the more qualified you become, the better opportunities you will have.

In addition to being fluent in at least two languages, some

of the most important qualities a translator/interpreter should possess are:

1. Confidentiality
2. Accuracy (with no omissions)
3. Impartiality
4. Professionalism

It is crucial that translators and interpreters maintain an impartial stance at all times. It used to be very common for anyone who was bilingual to be pulled into an interpreting situation on the spot, but increased regulations in numerous industries are making this much less common. And for good reason: a person who is not properly trained as an interpreter is not aware of the code of conduct that is expected in all situations.

For example, let's say an interpreter is called in to interpret the conversation at a medical appointment. The interpreter is required to express exactly what is being said in the conversation without inserting their own opinion or omitting details. Not only is it preferable to maintain an impartial attitude, but it is also actually required so that the interpreter stays within the law. Confidentiality is also paramount.

Imagine a situation where you are interpreting a conversation related to a topic you morally oppose (ending life support, abortion, and so on). If you accepted an assignment that dealt with one of these topics, you would be required to say exactly what the patient is saying, and with the same body language. So if a woman were vehemently asking for an abortion, you would have to be able to express that exactly the way she did. Interpreters are not allowed to omit or embellish, and you have to be okay with that.

Medical personnel and other professionals also must be careful to abide by the law regarding communicating with patients in other languages. As part of being impartial and providing a patient with the most complete information, a bilingual doctor is not allowed to speak to a patient in another language in a medical setting. By law, patients must be given the opportunity to have a qualified interpreter present who can relay the meaning of the conversation objectively. Also, medical facilities must provide an interpreter at no cost to the patient.

On the other hand, the opposite problem often exists when members of a patient's family attempt to interpret. They also have a vested interest in what happens with the patient, so their interpretations frequently omit important information. Also, properly communicating the nuances of medical terminology requires proper training and continual study on the part of the healthcare interpreter.

Nature of the Work

Interpreters and translators enable cross-cultural communication between people through the written and spoken word. This is important work, and it is not to be taken lightly. This doesn't mean that it's not satisfying and sometimes downright enjoyable, though.

As a cross-cultural advocate, interpreters and translators have the chance to make a difference in people's lives every day. Think of how important it is for anyone to have a qualified professional interpreter who speaks their native language when they suddenly find themselves in the hospital, for example. As a properly trained professional, you would become a lifeline for that person and be able to provide them with compassion and the security of knowing that they understand what is being said in their presence.

Skills Required

Translators and interpreters must be fluent in at least one or two languages other than their native language. They must continually expand their vocabulary and refine their abilities over time.

In fact, like many other professions, continuing education is a requirement for obtaining , maintaining, and renewing your interpretation and translation credentials and licenses.

Translators must be meticulous in their work, but they must also be able to capture the overall tone of a document and convey the exact message the original author intended. There is a certain amount of "art" to it, depending on the type of document. For example, a translator working on a fiction book would have to think more artistically than one who was working on a legal document.

Interpreters must have similar skills to translators, but they must also have people skills. Interpreters must accurately represent what a person is saying in terms of spoken language AND body language. Of course, having good people skills will make your job of interpreting much easier and effective. An interpreter who is professionally trained and who can make people feel comfortable in their presence will have a better chance of success in their career.

Aside from the basic skill of having proficiency in your languages, there are also numerous skills that you can enhance with special training. As I mentioned previously the demand for translators and interpreters continues to grow significantly year after year. Much of this demand is in specialized areas such as medicine, law, and education. The translator or interpreter who has completed additional training on translating for these specialized fields has an extra skillset in terms of vocabulary and specialized industry knowledge. Putting in the effort to educate yourself and get certified sets you apart from the average ad hoc bilingual interpreter.

Keep in mind it is becoming increasingly more difficult to find employment without proper credentials and such as certification as court or medical interpreter. Furthermore, private companies and government agencies' contracts usually require the most qualified interpreter and translator for a job, which means national certification whether you hold a master's or PhD level of education.

One thing to keep in mind is that it is always in your best interest to be objective, thorough, and accurate in your work because you never know who might be evaluating you. For example, the professional requesting your services may be fluent in the language you are interpreting, but they are not allowed to interfere with the conversation. They also may not let on how much of the language they understand.

Sometimes a second interpreter will be deliberately brought into a situation so that they can observe your work and give their professional opinion on the quality of your interpretation. In addition, you may find yourself interpreting for a person who has limited English proficiency, but it may be difficult to determine how much English they actually know when you first meet them. They may hold back how much they know on purpose, or they may simply not tell you. However, every once in a while such a person could potentially jump in and say something in English. So you have to be true to the art of interpreting.

Be aware that interpreters must recuse themselves from personal conflicts of interest. They must be unbiased, neutral, and impartial. These are all things that you learn when you go through training and certification. If you adhere to these policies, you can gain work, but if you do not, you won't endure very long in this career because you will be called out either by a client, a participant in a meeting, or perhaps by the contractor you are working with.

If you are on assignment and there is an extra person there just to supervise, they may be there to accompany that person to see how you work. Always assume that you are being listened to, and be aware that sometimes you are being recorded, whether in person, on the phone, or on a video chat. In court proceedings, everything is transcribed, so there will be records of everything you said. Therefore, precision, accuracy, and lack of omissions are very important so that you have the correct context of everything you are interpreting.

When you begin to assess the level of your own language skills, you may be surprised to discover how strong your base knowledge is or is not. You may need some language classes, grammar lessons, or other coursework and certifications to round out your credentials.

Assessments

By now you may be wondering if translating or interpreting is the right career choice for you and if so, which one is better suited to your skills and personality. I've designed this assessment to help guide you to determine which path may be right for you.

General Career Suitability Assessment

1. Do you have a thorough knowledge of two or more spoken languages, or of ASL?

   Y   N   not sure

2. Are you comfortable translating the exact meaning of a conversation or piece of text, even if it goes against your personal beliefs?

   Y   N   not sure

3. Can you refrain from adding extra meaning to a text or to a conversation?

   Y   N   not sure

4. Are you willing to uphold the highest ethical standards in your work?

   Y   N   not sure

5. Are you willing to keep improving your language skills and to stay current on industry trends and laws throughout your career?

   Y   N   not sure

6. Will you continually dedicate time, effort, and money toward obtaining your industry training and certifications?

   Y   N   not sure

Add up your score using the following scale:

Y = 5 points

N = 0 points

Not sure = 2 points

If you scored 24-30, you may be well suited to translation or interpretation work. (Please continue with the Translation vs. Interpretation Assessment to determine which career would be better suited to your personality.)

If you scored between 19 and 23, you may be suited for this profession if you decide to put in the hard work it requires.

If you scored below 18, then this industry is likely not a good fit for you at this time.

Translation vs. Interpretation Assessment

Congratulations! We have determined that a career in translation or interpretation may be a good fit for you. Now the question is, which one: translation or interpretation?

Answer the questions below to find out:

1. Do you enjoy working alone with your computer for extended periods of time?

   Y   N   not sure

2. Do you enjoy working with people most of the time?

   Y   N   not sure

3. Do you like a peaceful work environment?

   Y   N   not sure

4. Do you like a bustling, ever-changing work environment?

   Y   N   not sure

5. Do you prefer to have time to come up with the perfect words for a translation?

    Y   N   not sure

6. Do you enjoy the challenge of interpreting under pressure while other people are watching you and possibly evaluating the quality of your work on the spot?

    Y   N   not sure

7. Are you great at writing?

    Y   N   not sure

8. Do you consider yourself a "people person"?

    Y   N   not sure

9. Do you like having consistency in your work environment?

    Y   N   not sure

10. Can you maintain your composure when under stress (ex., in a courtroom, hospital, or natural disaster situation)?

    Y   N   not sure

Add up your score using the following scale:

For odd-numbered questions (1, 3, 5, 7, 9):

Y = 0 points

N = 5 points

Not sure = 3 points

Total for odd-numbered questions ____

For even-numbered questions (2, 4, 6, 8, 10),
Y = 5 points
N = 0 points
Not sure = 3 points
Total for even-numbered questions ____

Total for all 10 questions ____

If your total for all 10 questions is between 0 and 20, you are well suited for a career in translation.

If your total for all 10 questions is between 35 and 50, then you are well suited for a career in interpretation.

If your total score was between 21 and 34, then it is unclear which career best suits you. I recommend that you spend some time thinking about your true preferences and your ideal work environment, and then take the assessment again when you have gained more clarity on your personal needs and preferences. Perhaps a visit to a courtroom with an interpreter on the case or translating a two-page document may help you to decide.

CHAPTER 3

About Industry

Most In-demand Spoken Languages Around the World

The most in-demand spoken languages can move around, some from year to year, with their placement on the list, but in general they stay consistent. The top 10 spoken languages around the world are:

1.	Chinese-Mandarin	918 Million
2.	Spanish	480
3.	English	379
4.	Hindi and Urdu	341
5.	Arabic	290.0
6.	Bengali	228
7.	Portuguese	221
8.	Russian	154
9.	Japanese	128
10.	Western Punjabi	93 Million

Top languages by population Ethnologue (**2019, 22nd edition**)

The following languages are listed as having at least 10 million first language speakers in the 2019 edition of _Ethnologue_, a language reference published by SIL International, which is based in the United States.[7]

Earnings depend on the language, subject matter, skill, experience, education, certification, and type of employer; salaries of interpreters and translators can vary widely.

Interpreters and translators who know languages for which there is a greater demand, or that relatively few people can translate, often have higher earnings, as do those with specialized expertise.

Individuals classified as language specialists for the U.S. federal government earned an average of $87,889 annually in 2016. High-level conference interpreters working full time can earn more than $100,000 annually.

For those who are not salaried, earnings may fluctuate, depending on the availability of work. Freelance interpreters usually earn an hourly rate, whereas translators who freelance typically earn a rate per word, per hour, or a flat rate per project. Employment of interpreters and translators is projected to increase 20 percent over the 2019–2029 decade. This growth will be driven partly by strong demand in healthcare settings and work related to the United States Homeland Security. Note that the average job growth projection for 2019–2029 in most industries in the US is about 4 percent.

Note: All Occupations includes all occupations in the U.S. Economy.
Source: U.S. Bureau of Labor Statistics, Occupational Employment Statistics
Bureau of Labor Statistics, U.S. Department of Labor, *Occupational Outlook Handbook*, Interpreters and Translators, on the Internet at https://www.bls. gov/ooh/media-and-communication/interpreters-and-translators.htm **Last Modified Date:** Tuesday, September 1, 2020

Additionally, higher demand for interpreters and translators results directly from the broadening of international ties and the increase in the number of foreign-language speakers in the United States. Both trends are expected to continue, contributing to relatively rapid growth in the number of jobs for interpreters and translators. As for American Sign Language, there is also tremendous growth due to disability laws across the country. The public schools continually recruit ASL interpreters to work with their hard-of-hearing or impaired-hearing students.

Current events and changing political environments, often difficult to foresee, will increase the need for people who can work with other languages. For example, Homeland Security needs are expected to drive increasing demand for interpreters and translators of Middle Eastern and Northern African languages, primarily in federal government agencies such as the Department of Defense, the Justice Department, the FBI, ICE, TSA, etc.

Demand will remain strong for translators of the languages referred to as "PFIGS" (Portuguese, French, Italian, German, and Spanish), Arabic and Middle Eastern languages, and the principal Asian languages (Chinese, Japanese, and Korean).

As for the ASL, there is also tremendous growth due to disability laws across the country. Public schools K-12 and healthcare agencies continually recruit ASL interpreters to work with their hard-of-hearing or impaired-hearing students/patients.

Technology has made the work of interpreters and translators easier; however, note that technology is not likely to have

a negative impact on employment of interpreters and translators because such innovations are incapable of producing work
comparable to work produced by these human professionals.

Interpreters and translators are employed in a variety of
industries, reflecting the diversity of employment options in
the field. About 33 percent work in public and private educational institutions such as schools, colleges, and universities.
About 12 percent work in healthcare and social services assis-
tance, many of whom work in hospitals. Another 10 percent
work in areas of government such as federal, state, and local
courts. Other employers of interpreters and translators include
publishing, telephone companies, airlines, insurance companies, and interpreting and translating agencies. Yet about 22
percent of interpreters and translators are self-employed.

In 2017, the top five United States governmental agencies' budgets for T & I expenditures are:

1. Dept. of Defense   236 Million
2. Dept. of Justice   125 Million
3. Dept. of Homeland Security   54 Million
4. Dept. of State   42 Million
5. Dept. of Health & Human Services   14 Million

*15 Slator Article source; US Federal Gov 2017 Language Services Spending

USAspending.gov, which showed that for FY 2018, the
US government has awarded 4,005 contracts worth a total of
just over USD 100m.

This website is operated by the US Department of Treasury and created as a result of the Federal Funding Accountability and Transparency Act of 2006. The US government's financial year runs from October 1st to September 30th of the next year, so that's USD 100m awarded in just a little over four months. The top 10 contracts by value accounted for 40% of the total expenditure. The Department of Justice was the biggest spender, awarding a total of USD 40.3m and some 2,232 contracts. This was followed by the Department of Homeland Security with USD 27.3m and 186 contracts, then the Department of Defense with USD 10.2m and 78 contracts.

Top 10 US Government Translation & Interpretation Contract FY 2018

#	Value (USD)	Vendor	Agency
1	$7,500,000	SOS International LLC	Department of Justice
2	$7,000,000	CWU Inc	Department of Defense
3	$5,000,000	Language Line LLC	Department of Homeland Security
4	$4,038,840	Jerome Translation Group Inc.	Department of Homeland Security
5	$3,858,660	Jerome Translation Group Inc.	Department of Homeland Security
6	$2,957,400	Jerome Translation Group Inc.	Department of Homeland Security
7	$2,609,300	Language Line LLC	Department of Homeland Security
8	$2,449,700	Transperfect Translations	Department of Homeland Security
9	$2,380,178	Mid Atlantic Professionals Inc.	Department of State
10	$2,201,934	Mid Atlantic Professionals Inc.	Department of State

*Slator used the unique identifier called the "Parent Duns Numbers" as our reference to ensure we cover textual differences in company names and instances of subsidiaries belonging to the same parent company for the transaction counts. The count also considers modifications such as negative adjustments against contracts awarded at an earlier date due to the awarding agency exercising an option, the contract being completed early, or other reasons.

The Slator 2020 Language Industry Market Report provides a comprehensive view of the global language services and technology industry, which, according to Slator, grew to a USD 24.2bn market in 2019. The report presents analysis of survey data on both translation management systems (TMS) and machine translation (MT) technology.

Considering the current situation, Slator makes an early estimate that the coronavirus outbreak could lead to an 8% decline in the overall market over the course of 2020, before rebounding in 2021, with some industries and sub-industries affected worse than others. The report also presents a market outlook, which includes revised projections based on Slator's 2020 coronavirus impact assessment. Projected market growth to 2022 is USD 25.3bn.

Slator 2020 Language Industry Market Repot Data and Research May 1, 2020

American Sign Language (ASL)

American Sign Language (ASL) is important to the deaf and hard-of-hearing communities because that is their main method of communication. ASL is specific to the United States, and it is based on English. For example, the alphabet is the English alphabet. ASL is not universal.

The Registry of Interpreters for the Deaf, Inc. (RID), a national membership organization, plays a leading role in advocating for excellence in the delivery of interpretation and transliteration services between people who use sign language and people who speak English. In collaboration with the Deaf community, RID supports members and encourages the growth of the profession through the establishment of a national standard for qualified sign language interpreters and translators, ongoing professional development, and adherence to a code of professional conduct.

Certification

As with many vocations, certifications improve salaries for ASL interpreters. A professional certification from the Registry of Interpreters for the Deaf, or RID, can increase hourly wages to as much as $30 to $35 per hour, or $62,000 to $73,000 per year. A sign language interpreter at the CIA can earn anywhere from $75,000 to $116,000 per year with an RID and National Interpreter Certification.

Location

Besides certification, location influences pay. Due to the cost of living, certain markets just demand higher salaries to attract qualified candidates. Professionals on Long Island, NY, earn 35 percent more per year, so an RID-certified ASL interpreter will likely make $84,000 to $99,000 per year. The same can also be said for Boston, Massachusetts, where workers tend to make 32 percent more per year. In this city, an RID-certified ASL interpreter could make $81,840 to $96,360. But those working in Duluth, Minnesota, don't fare as well, earning 20 percent less than average. Now you're looking at salaries from $49,600 to $58,400, even with RID certification.[15] However, this salary is still competitive when you consider the required education and training versus job salary and work satisfaction.

In collaboration with the Deaf community, RID supports our members and encourages the growth of the profession through the establishment of a national standard for qualified sign language interpreters, ongoing professional development, and adherence to a code of professional conduct.

There is an ever-increasing need for ASL interpreters in the areas of education, law, and healthcare, as there are many laws and regulations that institutions, businesses, and medical offices need to comply with regarding providing clear information to those who cannot hear.[16]

The ASL interpreting industry is more well established

than the foreign language translating and interpreting industries, and it provides a good model to study.

The Registry of Interpreters for the Deaf strives to advocate for best practices in interpreting, professional development for practitioners, and for the highest standards in the provision of interpreting services for diverse users of languages that are signed or spoken.[9]

Alternative Pathway to Eligibility as of July 1, 2012

If you do not hold the necessary degree to take your exam, you may apply for the Alternative Pathway. The Alternative Pathway consists of an Educational Equivalency Application that uses a point system, awarding credit for college classes, interpreting experience, and professional development.

RID Certification

RID plays a leading role in establishing a national standard of quality for interpreters. RID certifications are a highly valued asset and provide an independent verification of an interpreter's knowledge and abilities, allowing them to be nationally recognized for the delivery of interpreting services among diverse users of signed and spoken languages. Furthermore, in some states, holding a valid RID certification is mandatory to provide interpreting services.

RID Certification Process

Each RID credential has unique requirements that must be completed before it can be awarded. Some certifications involve passing a series of exams and others involve submitting documentation of training and experience. In all cases, if the candidate is determined to meet or exceed RID's national standard, they are awarded certification.

RID Certifications – Registry of Interpreters for the Deaf

RID currently offers two different certifications. In addition, RID currently recognizes certifications that were previously offered by RID, but the exams are no longer available, as well as credentials assessed and awarded by the National Association of the Deaf (NAD). Individuals who hold NAD credentials that have been previously recognized by RID are considered certified members of RID.[10]

Work Environment

Interpreters work in a variety of settings, such as hospitals, courtrooms, and conference centers. They are required to travel to the site—whether it is in a neighboring town, or on the other side of the world—where their services are needed.

Interpreters who work over the phone, or via video, generally work in call centers and may keep a standard five-day, 40-hour workweek, unless they are a freelancer. Interpreters for deaf students in schools usually work in a school setting for nine months out of the year.

Translators usually work alone or in a small group, depending on the organization. They must frequently perform under the pressure of deadlines and tight schedules! Sometimes a document may need to be rendered in another language in a matter of minutes or hours. Some translators work in-house/on-site; others may choose to work from home. However, technology allows them to work from almost anywhere.

Typical Workday of a Translator

The typical workday of a translator can be different from day to day, especially depending on deadlines, but translators typically have much more regular workdays than interpreters. Translating work can require anywhere from a few hours to a few months on any given project, so there is still a great variety possible. Longer projects can provide a level of consistency for the translator.

Of course there are many relatively new tools to assist translators and to help speed up their work. Translators can use online references and computer software to start off their projects, if desired, but there is still a significant amount of thoughtful writing and editing involved.

Translators must be meticulous, and they must be careful not to rely too heavily on modern translation tools. If they do, their work will be subpar. Also, at least two translators are used on every document to ensure the quality of the work.

Translators should also be comfortable working for extended periods alone or in an office environment. Usually, someone who enjoys translating prefers some degree of solitude, as opposed to someone who works as an interpreter and has more variation in his or her daily work. They must also be comfortable with meeting new people and public speaking. You always have at least two listeners and sometimes many more or a large audience.

Typical Workday of an Interpreter

The work of interpreters varies a lot each day, and it varies by industry. The typical day of someone doing legal interpretation will be different from that of someone who is on staff at a school. Interpreters must be ready for a wide range of situations.

Interpreting can be intense at times, and you must be mentally prepared to be professional and objective. However, in addition you must also accurately convey the words in the proper context. Body language of the person for whom you are interpreting is also important with the intonation. Not only must you use words that exactly convey what the person is saying, but you must also gesture with the same level of enthusiasm, anger, etc. that the person is expressing.

The interpretation business is open twenty-four hours per day, seven days per week. If desired, you can work at any hour of the day; the flexibility to access work can be great for many professionals. Interpreters can find themselves in just about any scenario. For example, a patient may need help understanding the risks related to a medical procedure she is about to undergo. Or an angry parent may need help expressing themselves in a conversation about their student's grades or disciplinary problems at school. Other situations can be less serious, but generally, interpreting requires a certain amount of energy and stamina for a person to enjoy the work and to be effective. Assignments can last anywhere from 20 minutes to eight hours. Although, when an assignment is more than several hours, two interpreters may be assigned to alternate periodically to avoid fatigue and to maintain the integrity of the communication.

Education and Training

The educational backgrounds of interpreters and translators vary. Knowing at least two languages is essential. Although it is not necessary to have been raised bilingual to succeed, many interpreters and translators grew up speaking two languages, and others studied in school.

In high school, students can prepare for these careers by taking a broad range of courses that include English writing and comprehension, foreign languages, and basic computer proficiency.

Other helpful pursuits include spending time abroad, engaging in direct contact with other cultures, and reading extensively on a variety of subjects in English and at least one other language.

Employment and Earnings Outlook

Best Paying Cities for Interpreters and Translators

The highest paid in the interpreter and translator profession work in the metropolitan areas of Silver Spring, Maryland, District of Columbia, and Virginia Beach, Virginia. The Trenton, New Jersey, area also pays well, as does the city of San Francisco.[11]

Best Paying States for Interpreters and Translators

The states and districts that pay interpreters and translators the highest mean salary are the District of Columbia ($88,250), Virginia ($74,130), New Jersey ($69,190), Colorado ($67,510), and Maryland ($66,800).[12]

Interpretation

Types of Interpretation

Within the field of interpretation, there are several different methods that are used.

Consecutive Interpretation

Consecutive interpreting is where an interpreter listens to a section of speech and then summarizes it or relays the general meaning. This is primarily used in parent conferences at schools or medical appointments, business conference, and lectures. It could also be used in a setting such as a religious

35

service where the interpreter is working with a preacher, rabbi, etc. It is also common in the medical field and in certain school situations, like testing instructions or a report during an Individual Educational Plan (IEP) for Special Education students.

Simultaneous Interpretation

With simultaneous interpreting, the interpreter articulates what is being said in real time, while the person is still speaking. Such work can be quite taxing on the interpreter, so at least two interpreters will normally take turns speaking.

Simultaneous interpretation is often used in court and legal proceedings. It can be used in-person or via video conferences.

Face-to-Face Interpretation

Face-to-face interpretation simply means that the conversation is taking place in person. There could be face-to-face consecutive interpreting, or face-to-face simultaneous interpreting, for example, as with court interpretation, medical procedures, and conferences.

OPI- Over-the-Phone-Interpretation

OPI stands for over-the-phone interpreting, and it is commonly used by medical, customer services, and insurance companies to name a few. OPI is often used when there is an immediate need for an interpreter after standard business hours, although it is also used on a regular basis by many institutions and businesses, such as insurance, sales, and marketing companies.

Whispered Interpretation

Whispered interpreting usually requires special equipment, such as the type you see when interpreters are working for the United Nations. The interpreter often wears headphones and may be working from a soundproof booth. They speak in a low tone because there may be many different languages being spoken at the same time.

Nevertheless, if there is no special equipment available, they may in fact be whispering near the person they are relaying the interpretation to.

Categories of Interpreters

There are several categories of interpreters. Also, the skill level of interpreters can vary tremendously, so the more qualified you become, the more you will set yourself apart from others to get your career on track.

Certified Interpreter

This should be your ultimate goal as a professional interpreter or translator. You will have access to more work, higher salaries, and the ability to start your own T & I firm and qualify for federal, state, or local government contracts.

A certified interpreter is one who has gone through a formal certification process. There are many different certifications for different industries. For instance, the certification for medical interpreting is called CMI (Certified Medical Interpreter). Then there is C.O.R.E.-CHI, which means Certified in Health Care Interpreting. Both certifications are basically the same in terms of the level of expertise and credentialing; however, CMI is limited to certain languages, while C.O.R.E.-CHI is not language-specific.

Before you can sit for an exam, most certifications require an application and evaluation process so that your skill level may be assessed. Most require some work experience or significant volunteer experience. Once you qualify to sit for an exam, you must complete certain training before taking the test. For example, for C.O.R.E.-CHI, in order to qualify, you must still complete 40 hours of medical interpreter training. The training includes role-play exercises and passing a written exam.

Professionally Qualified Interpreter

Another way that interpreters may be categorized is by being "professionally qualified." This means that while they may not be officially certified by an entity, interpreters still have an impressive amount of experience interpreting in a professional environment. An example of such a person would be a doctor who practiced in a foreign country but who is now living in the United States. He/She could have vast experience interpreting in a medical setting as part of the work they did in their home country, or even after they came to the United States. Such a person would have a specialized, detailed knowledge of medical vocabulary in two or more different languages.

Language-Skilled/Ad Hoc Interpreter

A language-skilled/ad hoc interpreter is one who is usually not formally trained as an interpreter, but who has good language skills and has interpreted in various settings, whether at work or in social situations.

Such interpreters can be skilled in their work, but they cannot compare to the level of skill of a professionally qualified or certified interpreter.

Interpretation Jobs

There are as many types of interpretation as there are situations in life, but they generally break down into the following categories.

Legal

It is very common for an interpreter to be required for legal proceedings, and much of this need is driven by compliance with laws intended to protect the rights of the individual. Legal cases may involve judicial proceedings (which are in court) or quasi-judicial proceedings (which are held out of court but can be legally binding, as with arbitration and depositions).

Conference

Conference interpreters work at events that have multiple attendees, such as diplomatic gatherings, business conferences, and speaking events. There are often many languages being interpreted, and therefore many interpreters may be present.

Medical/Mental Health

In the medical and mental health fields, there are many laws and regulations that institutions must comply with regarding the rights of an individual patient.

An interpreter can be called on at any time of the day or night for such events, which are often serious and can be life-changing. Therefore, it is imperative that the interpreter be accurate while also being professional and remaining personally unaffected by the circumstances.

Escort

Escort interpreters travel or attend events with the speaker and stay by his side while interpreting. Such work can involve long trips or simply interpreting by someone's side for an hour or two.

School

Interpreters are often on staff at educational institutions. They can assist with parent/teacher conferences, Individual

Educational Plans, or 504 Plans as required by federal law under the ADA (Americans with Disabilities Act), when interpreting over the phone, or with students or parents who need clarification on a given topic. The need for school interpreters continues to increase as the American educational system becomes more immersed in diverse cultures.[13]

CHAPTER 4

The Role of Culture

Being Culturally Aware

While developing your skills as an interpreter, it is vital that you also practice sensitivity relative to other cultures. Many people spend most of their time immersed in the culture they grew up in, or the culture they're currently living in. Yet an effective interpreter must be able to work within the duality of understanding how both cultures operate and to then bring the two together. Linguistic and cultural assimilation and flexibility are the preferred combination in this profession.

Part of interpreting involves acting as a conduit, where you simply interpret what is being said by the other person. At the next level of cultural understanding, there is the cultural broker who helps people understand where the point of view of the speaker is coming from. For example, an interpreter in a medical setting would be showing cultural sensitivity if they were familiar with home remedies commonly used in the patient's home country.

Interpreters who are culturally aware may also find themselves serving as an advocate for the speaker. For example, there could be a patient in a medical situation who is simply nodding in agreement to everything the doctor is saying; this is not necessarily a sign of understanding.

What if the patient is from a culture where it is frowned upon to ask questions of medical personnel? What if the patient's education level is not sufficient for them to fully understand what is going on based on what the doctor has said?

So as we reference being culturally aware, we're talking about diversity in terms of understanding cultural sensitivity toward others from different upbringings, countries, religious affiliation, even from protocol in terms of addressing gender in certain cultures. For example, you don't shake hands with women in certain cultures. Or that we should not address people by their first name unless we're given permission to do so; instead, we would stick to their title—mister, doctor, professor, engineer, ambassador, and so on.

These things are critical in terms of how we're able to bridge the cultural gap, and they lead to better cultural understanding because often, as English speakers or Americans in particular, we tend to have our own ideology in terms of how we broker deals, how we run meetings, or how we invite guests to events, while not realizing that in many cultures it takes a process before they warm up to it. Various cultures around the world can be more reserved, but we are more open in terms of how we let folks in. Sometimes we are more diplomatic, with more protocol than other countries.

We have to understand that when we're discussing personal things, like someone's immigration or medical status, these are extremely personal topics. People are usually, in various cultures, not accustomed to having a third party who they don't know involved in their personal medical care or in their personal business. Even though they may have a need for it, as an interpreter you are still a stranger. So recognize your role as that stranger who is involved in someone's personal care, business, medical history, or legal status, for immigration, for example. You're privy to a lot of confidential and delicate information.

We know, as interpreters and translators, we have a confidentiality clause that is part of our daily work, meaning that we cannot divulge any information. We have to take that seriously, and that's why it's important to go through training that indoctrinates you in terms of understanding the code of ethics and your role, so that you're not in violation of anyone's rights nor your professional Code of Conduct.

Business Etiquette

Another important area where culture plays a large role is in business transactions. The way business dealings are conducted from country to country varies tremendously. For instance, in certain regions, it is completely acceptable to arrive half an hour or an hour late for an appointment. In other countries, it is crucial to allow for some social time before starting to talk business. Such acts might be considered inefficient or confusing to an American businessperson, but it's always important to remember that there is no one right or wrong way to conduct business. When you educate yourself on cultural differences, you will be a far more effective interpreter.

It's important to understand that we, as Americans, can often be seen as pushy; because of this, we may lose out on deals. We sometimes unintentionally push people away because we don't understand their culture, customs, and traditions.

Then there are other simpler things we might not be aware of. For example, in some cultures, you may be insulting a person if you cross your legs in front of them because doing so exposes the bottom of your shoe. Or when a man goes to shake a woman's hand. There are little nuances and little things, and if you're unaware of them, you're going to make a big mistake in words alone. And then you will wonder why you didn't get the contract. You had everything laid out, and the money was good, and everything would have been fine, but you didn't know how to deal with your potential client. You didn't know how to approach them, and you weren't sensitive to their culture.

As Americans, we are very strict about being on time, and that's fine, but you have to be aware it is not the same case in some cultures.

In addition, in some cultures, it is common for nothing business related to be discussed during the first meeting. Instead, the priority is on getting to know one another and discussing family, travels, and so on. You have to know how to engage with people from other cultures in order to win them over.

As Americans, we tend to be overly polished and formal with our business etiquette, and we need to learn how to tone this down when presented with a different culture. In many cultures, you will never win over a business with fast-talking, big proposals and other overwhelming tactics. It's important to approach these things gradually.

CHAPTER 5

Rules & Regulations

United States Laws & Regulations Affecting the Industry

Changes to laws and statutes can have a significant impact on the translating and interpreting industry. In the U.S., there are many personal rights that are protected by law, which means that translators and interpreters are often called upon to provide services so that businesses and institutions can stay compliant with current regulations.

When such services are required, the entity that is required to maintain compliance is also the entity that pays for the translators' and interpreters' fees. Many places maintain a regular pool of translators and interpreters who either work in-house or who they call on regularly to assist with maintaining compliance. This is very good news for those of you who work in this industry because you are certain to get paid, even if the person for whom you are scheduled to interpret does not show up!

Think of all the places that are affected by laws that protect personal rights: for example, courts, schools, and medical facilities...the list goes on and on.

Individual Right to a Fair Trial

One right that we are all familiar with is an individual's right to a fair trial. We often think about this in terms of being able to have a trial before a jury of our peers, but there is much more to it than that. For the person who does not speak English as a first language, the law requires that an interpreter be made available so that they can fully understand what is going on in the courtroom and in other related legal scenarios.

Section 1557

"Section 1557 is the civil rights provision of the Affordable Care Act of 2010. Section 1557 prohibits discrimination on the grounds of race, color, national origin, sex, age, or disability in certain health programs and activities. The Section 1557 final rule applies to any health program or activity, any part of which receives funding from the Department of Health and Human Services (HHS), such as hospitals that accept Medicare, or doctors who receive Medicaid payments; the Health Insurance Marketplaces and issuers that participate in those Marketplaces; and any health program that HHS itself administers.

Protections for Individuals with Limited English Proficiency

Consistent with longstanding principles under civil rights laws, the final rule makes clear that the prohibition on national origin discrimination requires covered entities to take reasonable steps to provide meaningful access to each.[14]

Getting Hired

How to Properly Prepare Yourself

In order to be successful in this industry, you must invest in yourself. How much training and education you need depends on your background and experience level, but everyone needs to be willing to continually educate and improve themselves. In fact, all certification programs require continuing education units (CEUs) to maintain ongoing certification.

This career is for those who are serious about it. Either you want to do it as a full-time career, or you want to do it as a part-time career, but either way, it's still a career! And you can work for a company or start your own business.

What Type of Education Do Interpreters and Translators Need?

In 2012, the Registry of Interpreters for the Deaf gave a more formal coating to the process of becoming a nationally certified interpreter, requiring aspiring hearing interpreters to have a bachelor's degree before testing. Other organizations, such as the American Translators Association and the International Association of Conference Interpreters, offer various forms of certification as well. Given the formal education, certification, and state regulations, becoming an interpreter and translator can be an involved process. While a formal education is becoming increasingly important, those seeking to enter the field must, above all else, be fluent in English and another language.

You're going to need to invest in training, certifications, licenses, and required tests. And all this costs money, but when you compare it to the cost of college education, it's no contest. If you follow my guidance and work hard, you can usually get a 100 percent return on investment in under a year.

As far as testing and certifications, you will need to know when exams will be given by the accreditation board in your state. Many tests are given twice a year or quarterly, but it all depends on the state. Also, it's important to know that you have to qualify before you can even sit for certain exams. There are prerequisites. Depending on your beginning skill level and on what state you live in, you could become trained and certified in as soon as three months, or it could take closer to a year. Usually, I see candidates complete certification in six to nine months.

Becoming certified increases your employment opportunities exponentially! I have personally obtained two national interpreting and linguistics certifications within a 90-day period, and I have trained others to successfully do so as well. Some organizations will hire you and give you a probationary period to get your credentials in order. It depends on what the potential client needs and how well that pairs with your skills.

In such a situation, the employer will usually do a pre-assessment. If you have good results, that is enough for you to remain with the employer until you can get the required credentials in order. Sometimes they will even pay for you to go get additional training and certifications so that their organization can stay in compliance with federal, state, and local laws or their clients.

How to Get a Job as an Interpreter and Translator

Internships are a great way to gain valuable work experience and give your résumé greater appeal. Volunteering, working alongside more experienced interpreters, and networking with those already established in the field are also excellent avenues for bolstering your job prospects. Some interpreters create their own job market by building a freelance practice. Occasionally, they will contact agencies for outside assignments as an independent contractor.

Job Satisfaction

Average Americans work well into their 60s, so workers might as well have a job that's enjoyable and a career that's fulfilling. A job with good work-life balance and solid prospects to improve, get promoted, and earn a higher salary would make many employees happy. Here's how interpreters' and translators' job satisfaction is rated in terms of upward mobility, stress level, and flexibility:[15]

- Upward Mobility (Opportunities for advancements and salary): Average to High
- Stress Level (Work environment and complexities of the job's responsibilities): Average
- Flexibility (Alternative working schedule and work-life balance): High

Common Mistakes

Here are some common mistakes people make when trying to get hired:

1. Candidates assume that being bilingual is sufficient and puts you in a good position to be hired. The truth is that you have to not only be bilingual and proficient in both languages, fluently and equally, but you also have to have the skillset for interpretation or translation. You need training in the form of seminars, classes, and/or certifications to help you acquire specific skills.

2. Candidates are not prepared to do on-the-spot translation or interpretation during the interview. Being asked to perform during the interview can really throw candidates off, especially if they are not familiar with the terminology used in the given topic. As a translator or interpreter, you will work in a field of specialty, and you should continually build and enrich your linguistic knowledge by collecting and studying glossaries, vocabulary collections, and industry-specific terminology to keep up with the changes in language and culture that are taking place around the globe. Be prepared to translate or role-play during your interview.

3. Candidates have not familiarized themselves with nuances related to geography. Depending on what region or country you are in, the vocabulary for a given language changes. For example, in Peru or Chile, there

are significant differences in the meanings of the same words compared to what you might hear in Mexico or Spain. These differences are very important, and if you are not careful, you can find yourself in big trouble having insulted someone by mistake!

4. Candidates are not familiar with the Code of Ethics they are required to abide by. There are specific rules and dos and don'ts for interpreters. Only by going through proper training will you be informed and come to understand your role as an interpreter.

5. Candidates do not have proper credentials. Even the most educated, fluent bilingual speakers may lose out on valuable job opportunities if they do not have the proper skills and credentials. Educate yourself on what employers are looking for, and come to the interview prepared.

6. Candidates use words from other languages when they translate or interpret. For example, when role-playing an interpreting session, some people will substitute words from their native language or from other languages in place of the correct word in the target language. Granted, there are cases where there is no equivalent in the target language, but in that case, you should be able to break down the meaning and convey it using words that do exist and that the person on the receiving end will completely understand.

7. Candidates are too immersed in one culture. While most people have one culture that is more familiar to them and to which they can relate, it's crucial to have the duality of understanding how both cultures operate. Then you can bring the two together and provide the best service you can.

Conclusion

In closing, I would like to offer the following advice; work smart and follow the guidelines in this book. You will undoubtly save some time, effort and money. I hope in reading this book that you have learned how to either jumpstart or how to get to the next level in the Translation and Interpretation industry by diversifiying your skills.

Look for my trainings and online courses about certifications for intepreters and translators.

Follow me on:

Twitter at https://twitter at /4ulanguages

LinkedIN https://www.linkedin.com/in/lynnhenryroach/.

In a world where you can be anything. Be your best SELF.

Glossary

ASL – American Sign Language

C.O.R.E.-CHI – Certified in Health Care Interpreting

Certified Interpreter – An interpreter who has gone through a formal certification process.

CMI – Certified Medical Interpreter

IMF – International Monetary Fund

Interpreter – One who translates spoken words.

Language Skilled/Ad Hoc Interpreter – One who is usually not formally trained as an interpreter, but who has good language skills and has interpreted in various settings.

Localization – Translating a language into the local dialect.

Machine Translation – Translation that is done by computers.

Professionally Qualified Interpreter – An interpreter who is not officially certified, but who also has an impressive amount of experience interpreting in a professional environment.

RID – Registry of Interpreters for the Deaf

Section 1557 – The Civil Rights provision of the Affordable Care Act of 2010.

Sight Translation – Where a short document is presented to an interpreter for them to read and translate orally on the spot.

Translator – One who translates written words.

WHO – World Health Organization

Index

D

E

S

Bibliography

Printed version: PDF Publication Date: 5/18/2016 Agencies:
Department of Health and Human Services Office of the
Secretary Effective Date: 7/18/2016 Document Type: rule
Document Citation: 81 FR 31375 Page: 31375-31473(99
pages) CFR: 45 CFR 92 RIN: 0945-AA02
Document Number: 2016-11458

Bureau of Labor Statistics, U.S. Department of Labor, Occupational
Outlook Handbook, Interpreters and Translators,
(visited *December 14, 2020*)
https://www.bls.gov/ooh/media-and-communication/in-
terpreters-and- translators.htm

Payne, Neil MD of "Cross Cultural Communication Consultancy,"
Kwintessential
www.kwintessential.co.uk/translation/interpretation.html
(visited January 2, 2021).
https://www.translationdirectory.com/article307.htm

"IBISWorld iExpert Industry Summary 54193
Translation Services in the US"
IBISWORLD.COM June 2014
www.ibisworld.com

International Association of Conference Interpreters
https://aiic.net/page/6244/imf-international-monetaryfund/
lang/1
March 12, 2018 www.aiic.org

Content created by the Office for Civil Rights (OCR)
https://www.hhs.gov/sites/default/files/1557-final-rule-
factsheet.pdf
June 12, 2020 https://www.hhs.gov/civil-rights

Report by the Secretariat World Health Organization
"Multilingualism: plan of action"
EXECUTIVE BOARD 121st Session (19 April 2007)
Provisional agenda item 6.3.
https://apps.who.int/gb/archive/pdf_files/EB121/B121_6-
en.pdf